W9-ADG-024

Jones Library, Inc.
43 Amity Street
Amherst, MA 01002

WITHDRAWN

What's Inside Me?
My Lungs

Dana Meachen Rau

MARSHALL CAVENDISH
NEW YORK

My Lungs

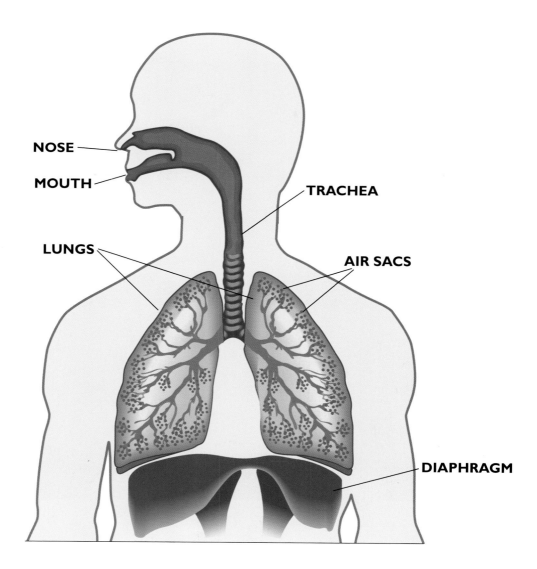

NOSE

MOUTH

TRACHEA

LUNGS

AIR SACS

DIAPHRAGM

Take a deep breath. Fresh air feels good on a summer day.

Air is all around you. It is filled with *oxygen*.

You need oxygen to use your brain. You need it to move your arms and legs. Every part of your body needs oxygen to do its job.

Your body takes in oxygen by breathing. Your body breathes all the time.

Air also has *carbon dioxide*. Your body makes carbon dioxide. When you breathe out, your body is getting rid of carbon dioxide.

You hold your breath when you swim underwater. You can stay underwater for only a short time. Your body needs air.

Your lungs are like two spongy balloons inside your chest. They fill up with air every time you breathe in.

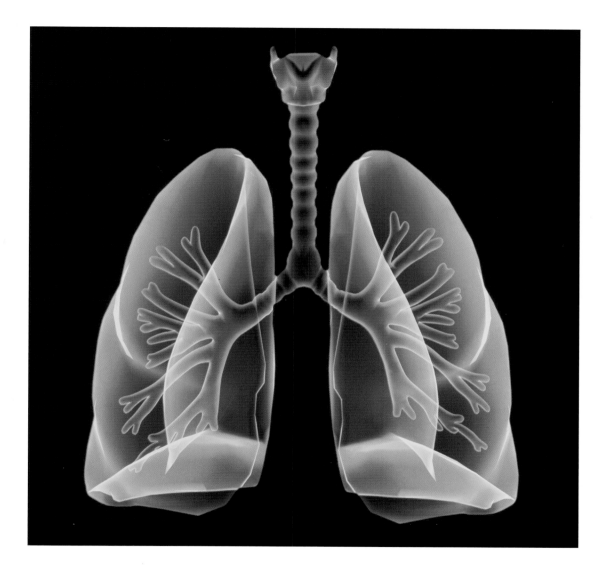

How does air get to your lungs? First it comes into your body through your mouth or nose.

You have hairs inside your nose. You also have *mucus*. These hairs and mucus trap dust so it will not go into your body.

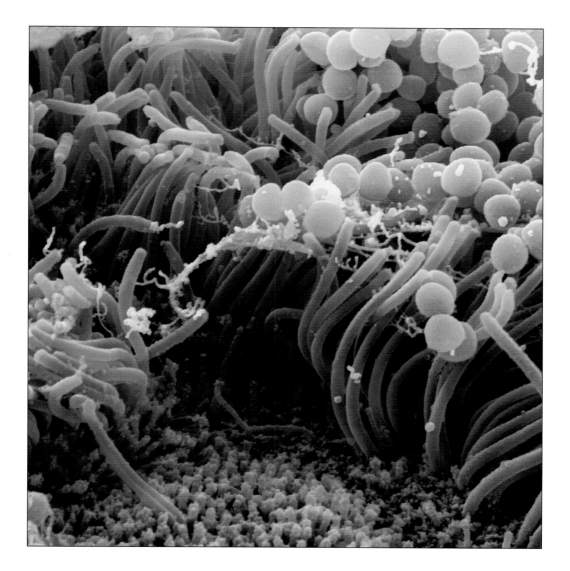

15

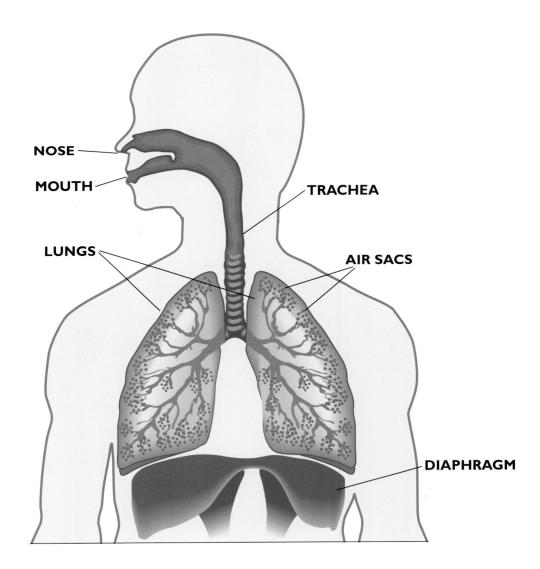

NOSE

MOUTH

TRACHEA

LUNGS

AIR SACS

DIAPHRAGM

Next the air travels down a tube called the *trachea*, or windpipe. Your trachea splits into two tubes. Each tube goes to a lung.

Inside your lungs, the tubes keep splitting. They look like branches on an upside-down tree.

There are groups of tiny *air sacs* at the end of each branch. The air sacs fill up with air. They look like bunches of tiny grapes.

There are more than 300 million air sacs in each of your lungs.

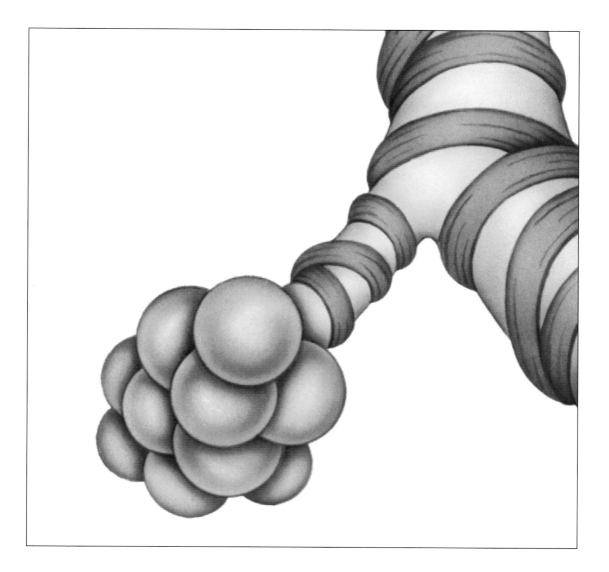

19

Oxygen moves from the air sacs into your blood. Your blood carries oxygen all around your body.

Carbon dioxide from your blood goes into the air sacs. It travels back up the tubes and out of your mouth or nose when you breathe out.

Your lungs get very large when you *inhale*. There is a muscle under your lungs called the *diaphragm*. It becomes flat to make room for the air in your lungs.

The diaphragm moves upward when you *exhale*. This helps push the air out of your lungs.

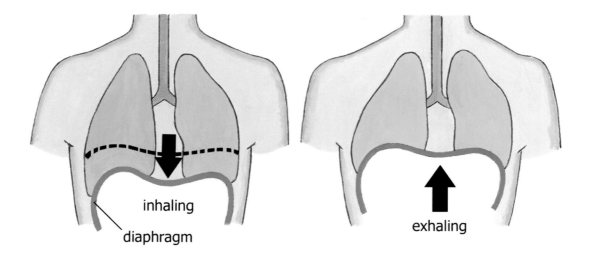

inhaling

diaphragm

exhaling

Sometimes dust gets into your lungs. *Coughing* is the way your body gets dust out. A cough is a burst of air that rushes from your lungs and out of your mouth.

Sneezing is another way your body gets rid of dust. Air from the lungs bursts out of your nose.

Every breath you take makes your body strong. Your lungs work hard to give your body the oxygen it needs to live.

Challenge Words

air sacs—Tiny balloons inside your lungs.

carbon dioxide (KAR-buhn die-OK-side)—The part of air your body does not need.

coughing—A burst of air from your lungs out your mouth.

diaphragm (DIE-uh-fram)—A muscle under your lungs.

exhale—To breathe out.

inhale—To breathe in.

mucus (MYOO-kuhs)—A sticky material in your nose.

oxygen (OK-si-juhn)—The part of air your body needs to work.

sneezing—A burst of air from your lungs out your nose.

trachea (TRAY-kee-uh)—The tube from your mouth to your lungs.

Index

Page numbers in **boldface** are illustrations.

air, 5, 8, 22
  pathway, 14, **16**
air sacs, **16**, 18, **19**, 21

brain, 6
breath, 28
  breathing in, **4**, 5, 6, 22, **23**
  breathing out, 8, **9**, **20**, 21, 22, **23**
  holding, **10**, 11

carbon dioxide, 8, 21
coughing, **24**, 25

diaphragm, **16**, 22, **23**
dust, 14, 25

exhaling, 8, **9**, **20**, 21, 22, **23**

hairs, 14, **15**

inhaling, **4**, 5, 6, 22, **23**

lungs, 12, **13**, **16**, 22, 28

mouth, **9**, 15, **16**, 21, **21**, **24**, 25
moving, 6, **7**, **29**
mucus, 14

nose, **2**, 14, **15**, 21, 26, **27**

oxygen, 5–6, 21, 28

sneezing, 26, **27**
strength, 28
swimming, **10**, 11

trachea, **16**, 17, 21

With thanks to Nanci Vargus, Ed.D.
and Beth Walker Gambro, reading consultants

Benchmark Books
Marshall Cavendish
99 White Plains Road
Tarrytown, New York 10591-9001
www.marshallcavendish.com

Text copyright © 2005 by Marshall Cavendish Corporation

All rights reserved. No part of this book may be reproduced or utilized in any form or by any means
electronic or mechanical, including photocopying, recording, or by any information storage and retrieval system,
without written permission from the copyright holders.

Library of Congress Cataloging-in-Publication Data

Rau, Dana Meachen, 1971–
My lungs / by Dana Meachen Rau.
p. cm. — (Bookworms: What's inside me?)
Includes index.
ISBN 0-7614-1780-X
1. Respiratory organs—Juvenile literature. I. Title. II. Series.

QP121.R35 2004
612.2—dc22
2004002517

Photo Research by Anne Burns Images

Cover photo by Corbis/Norbert Schaefer

The photographs in this book are used with the permission and through the courtesy of:
Corbis: pp. 1, 9, 20 Norbert Schaefer; p. 7 Jim Craigmyle; p. 10 Jim Cummins; p. 29 LWA-Dann Tardif.
Jay Mallin: p. 2. Visuals Unlimited: p. 4 Pegasus. Photo Researchers, Inc.: p. 13
Alfred Pasieka/Science PhotoLibrary; p. 15 Science Photo Library; p. 24 Carolyn A. McKeone;
p. 27 Damien Lovegrove/Science Photo Library. Custom Medical Stock Photo: pp. 19, 23.

Series design by Becky Terhune

Printed in China
1 3 5 6 4 2